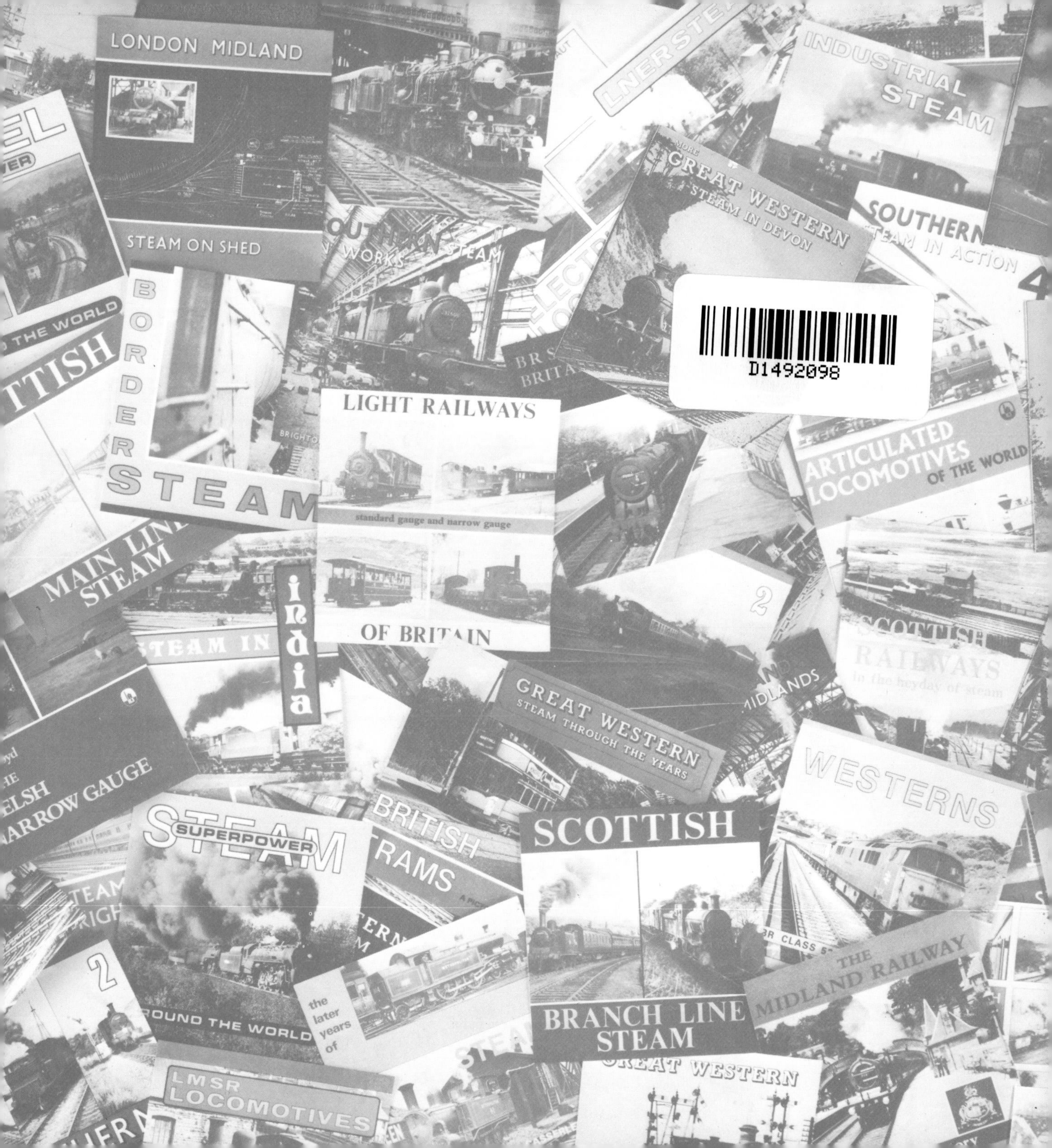

LONDON MIDLAND

STEAM ON SHED

LNER STEAM

INDUSTRIAL STEAM

SOUTHERN STEAM IN ACTION 4

GREAT WESTERN STEAM IN DEVON

BORDER STEAM

O THE WORLD

TTISH

MAIN LINE STEAM

STEAM IN india

LIGHT RAILWAYS

standard gauge and narrow gauge

OF BRITAIN

ARTICULATED LOCOMOTIVES OF THE WORLD

SCOTTISH RAILWAYS In the heyday of steam

2

GREAT WESTERN STEAM THROUGH THE YEARS

WESTERNS

NARROW GAUGE

SUPERPOWER STEAM

BRITISH TRAMS

SCOTTISH

THE MIDLAND RAILWAY

2

ROUND THE WORLD

the later years of

BRANCH LINE STEAM

GREAT WESTERN

LMSR LOCOMOTIVES

B R STANDARD CLASS 9F

BR STANDARD CLASS 9F

a study of British Railways Standard Class 9F 2-10-0 heavy freight locomotive

edited by G. Weekes

D. BRADFORD BARTON LTD

Frontispiece: Class 9F No. 92210 entering Evercreech Junction on the Somerset & Dorset with a southbound train on 31 July 1962—a photograph taken from the north-bound 'Pines Express'. The 9Fs became quite celebrated for passenger working over the fierce grades of this line; that this was only in the summer months, due to their not being fitted for train heating, was not as big a disadvantage as it might have been, for passenger traffic between Bath and Bournemouth was concentrated into that period to a large extent.   [P. J. Lynch]

© copyright D. Bradford Barton Ltd 1975 ☐ ISBN 0 85153 187 3 ☐ Set in Monotype Bembo and printed by offset litho by H. E. Warne Ltd, of London and St. Austell, for the publishers D. Bradford Barton Ltd, of Trethellan House, Truro, Cornwall

Following the nationalisation of Britain's railways in January 1948, twelve types of standard steam locomotives were designed and built under British Railways' auspices. These ranged from Pacifics, through 4-6-0s, Moguls, various tank engines of 2-6-2 and 2-6-4 wheel arrangement, to a heavy 2-10-0 for freight use. These B.R. Standard designs were built from 1951 to 1960, the last named 2-10-0s being known as Class 9F. They were the most numerous and also the last of the entire series, built in batches from 1953 through to the early months of 1960.

The basic concept of the Class 9 had been as a 2-8-2 but the extra weight available for adhesion with a 2-10-0 was the deciding factor which won the day for the latter layout. There was a crying need in the early 1950s on several of the Regions for a heavy up-to-date freight locomotive capable of reasonably fast running, and yet able to handle loose-coupled mineral trains of 1000 tons and more. The latter was in fact the original concept of the 'Nines'.

As with all the Standard designs, the overriding factors affecting the design were the need for simplicity, both in construction and in maintenance, allied to efficiency in operation. As a glance at a 9F shows, the combination of a wide fire-box, 5′ diameter coupled wheels and a massive boiler strained the L^2 loading gauge to its absolute limit. At this point, one may stress that any ten-coupled design in Britain had been rare in the extreme to this date, consisting of only the single GE 'decapod' tank and the famous 'Big Bertha' 0-10-0 on Lickey.

Two works were responsible for building the class—Crewe and Swindon, the former produced 198 in all, during the six years from 1953-58, whilst Western Region at Swindon turned out 53 of the class, from 1956-60—concurrently, as a point of interest, with the

'Warship' diesel-hydraulics. From 1958 onwards, it is interesting to note, building of all other classes had ceased, with the initial onset of the dieselisation programme.

In service the 9Fs proved trouble-free—after the curing of initial throttle problems with the first few produced—as was reflected in the steady building programme throughout the late 1950s. The first engines went to Western Region, followed by successive batches to London Midland and Eastern Regions, plus a few for special duties on the then existing North Eastern Region. Southern Region had no allocation—although five were later transferred there—while Scottish Region had a few, but only for a brief period.

The free-steaming quality of the design—with all but the worst of firemen—was allied to an ability to run extremely fast, as enginemen on all Regions soon found. Not long after their introduction, certainly by 1956, it had become well known that 9Fs could easily attain 80 and even 90 mph under favourable conditions, and that at these express speeds riding was still smooth and safe. Once again the adage was proved that small driving wheels were no bar to high speeds providing an engine had a good front-end. The story of the encroachment of what had been designed entirely as a heavy freight engine on to fast passenger working on quite a widespread scale is an interesting aspect of 9F history. As shed-masters began to realise the class would run fast and well on summer specials and long distance excursions, 'Nines' began to appear more and more on such turns; in the late 1950s they could be seen, for example, at Blackpool and Llandudno, on LM Region, alongside the more usual 'Black Fives', and on Western Region at Paignton and Plymouth. On the former Great Central Route, they were even rostered for regular working on expresses such as 'The Master Cutler' and 'The South Yorkshireman' for a time. Fast running by exuberant drivers, however, brought exorbitant wear in the cylinders and other running gear, bringing down the period between shed overhauls to a quite unacceptable mileage. This was inevitable, however, for no design could withstand what was basically misuse. Accordingly, a decree went out in 1959 that the use of 9Fs on passenger work was officially discouraged. On cross-country routes, notably the Somerset & Dorset, their use was allowed and the part played by 'Nines' over this hard—and in summer, heavily used—road was an interesting one.

The last three of the class were turned out from Swindon in the early part of 1960, including No. 92220, which was named *Evening Star*. Withdrawal of the first sixteen in the class began in 1964, from Eastern Region, followed by 65 in the following year, principally from Western Region where dieselisation was almost complete. LM Region was the last to retain 9Fs, the major batch of withdrawals occurring at the end of 1967. The final eighteen, based upon sheds in the north-west, were withdrawn the following summer.

Relatively few of the 251 9Fs differed from the normal specification of the class, the most notable being the Crosti-boilered batch . These variants are described in the captions which follow and it suffices here to say that all were aimed at cost saving, primarily to increase ability to work on cheaper, lower-grade coal. The Crosti pre-heater, the Giesl exhaust ejector, and the power stokers were all tried with this aim in mind. The Berkley mechanical stokers fitted to Nos. 92165-67 in 1958 were also a bid to do away with hand-firing, though introduced in far too half-hearted a way to be successful. Experience had shown that two good firemen were necessary to work a 9F anywhere near its limit for a sustained period on fast freights with little or no lay-by time, but 1958 was far too late in the day to introduce mechanical stoking. The grate area, too, was well below the optimum for mechanical stoking and after three or four years of use, principally on fitted freights between the Midlands and Carlisle, the five Saltley-allocated stoker-fired 9Fs reverted to normal hand firing. Tender variations, to suit differing regional operational requirements, are also detailed in the captions hereafter, four main types being fitted.

A minor point of interest worthy of note with the 9Fs was their wholehearted acceptance by footplate crews on all Regions, in contrast to the B.R. Pacifics from the same design stable. The introduction of the latter gave rise to mixed feelings, amounting to downright hostility in certain quarters on Western Region; but the 9Fs, although no less alien, were quite rapidly and cheerfully accepted. Despite lefthand drive, a big modern cab, and an appearance quite out of keeping with any Swindon product, few ex-GW enginemen opted for a 38xx on any duty when they had the choice of that or a 9F.

Swindon's own especial contribution to the 9F, other than at the design stage, was the double blastpipe and chimney fitted to the later W.R.-built units in the class. This was from 1958 onwards, following trials, both at the test plant and on the road, with No. 92178, resulting in a considerable improvement in performance. At the same time as these trials, the usual smoke deflectors were omitted from this locomotive to see whether these were still necessary after these revised draughting arrangements. Lack of the big sideplates made for an appearance even more handsome than was the case with them but practical considerations obviously outweighed this and No. 92178 soon reverted to standard. Under certain conditions of running, smoke drifted and badly obscured the outlook from the cab and on Western Region this made sighting particularly difficult in view of the driving position being on what was, to Swindon, the wrong side.

Looking back in time, the B.R. Standard 9Fs can fairly be classed as the best heavyweight all-rounder ever produced in Britain, and completely suited to the traffic requirements of the 1950s. For more specialised duties there were many better but considering the wide range of work undertaken by the 9Fs, they had no equal, let alone a peer. What other single class—from the Great Western, Southern, L.M.S., or L.N.E.R. or their forerunners— would have been at home on accepted 9F turns; loose-coupled mineral trains in the east Midlands and fast, fitted van trains over Shap; iron ore trains to Consett or Ebbw Vale and cross-country passenger services on the Somerset & Dorset; summer Saturday extras to North Wales or South Devon, and banking on Lickey; excursions to Blackpool and oil trains to Fawley; and above all, the day-in day-out freight turns everywhere that were the revenue-earning backbone of B.R. in the dying days of steam.

Those who judge steam locomotives by pre-war standards may dismiss the 'Nines' as utilitarian, as indeed they were. But it must be remembered times had changed; on the shed, on the road, on the footplate, and it took a rugged 'no-frills' design to survive on mixed traffic duties in the last rough-and-tumble decade of steam on Britain's railways.

Second of the Class 9Fs to be turned out was No. 92001, built at Crewe in 1953 and entering service early in 1954. She is seen here in Western Region service, at Ebbw Junction Shed (Newport), still with the original single blast pipe and chimney, later replaced by a double. The first six 9Fs were allocated to South Wales, for working heavy iron-ore trains—and gave minor initial trouble in service with regulators sticking open under certain conditions. To have the throttle immovably open on a 140-ton 2-10-0 was, to say the least, unnerving to a driver; fortunately minor modifications soon cured this trouble.

[Norman E. Preedy]

No. 92002 on shed at Crewe South, after moving from the Western to L.M. Region. The overall design of the class was admirably suited to the requirements of the 1950s—big enough to handle everything asked of them without being overworked; rugged enough to put up with an era of declining standards on shed; steaming well enough to withstand poor coal and 'green' firemen; fast enough for use in a virtually mixed-traffic capacity, and all with a route availability that was little short of astonishing for a ten-coupled machine. They had all the virtues of the other BR Standard designs and none of their drawbacks, resulting in widespread acceptance of them amongst enginemen on all Regions—even some of the diehards on the Western. [J. R. Carter]

No. 92207 was one of the later Swindon-built 9Fs, and is seen here outside the works on 24 May 1959 shortly before entering service. By this date, a double chimney was standard on new locomotives. Below, No. 92060, turned out from Crewe in 1955, with 1B Class tender (curved sides: holding 7 tons of coal and 4725 gallons of water), in September 1963. She was the first of the 9Fs allocated to Tyne Dock shed for Consett ore trains.   [Norman E. Preedy]

A close-up of the motion of No. 92054 at Lostock Hall in April 1968. By this date, when steam lingered on at only a few L.M. sheds in the north-west, and diesels had taken over the majority of B.R. workings, only rugged engines which could continue to give service under adverse conditions of maintenance remained in service.

[David M. Cox]

Walschaerts valve gear was inevitable on the 9Fs as on most of the other BR Standard designs, utilising three-bar slidebars and extremely long-lap, lap-travel valves—the latter being responsible for giving the class much of its ability for free running. Cylinders, 20″ diameter by 28″ stroke, were of similar dimensions to the Class 7 'Britannias'. This is one of the later W.R. 9Fs fitted by Swindon with a double chimney.   [Norman E. Preedy]

Double-chimneyed No. 92191, newly built at Swindon in 1958, awaits her 1F tender. Some of the W.R.-built batch of this period were allocated to Eastern Region, whilst contemporary ones from Crewe Works came down to enter service on Western Region.

[A. R. Butcher]

The front end of No. 92118 inside Didcot shed, 21 March 1965. Visible are the vertical coil-bearing springs and also the horizontal ones for side control on the pony truck, the general design of this latter following that of the B.R. Standard tanks.

[David M. Cox]

No. 92051 at Carlisle (Kingmoor) in April 1967, framed between Class 20 and 25 diesels. She has one of the bigger high-sided tenders that were usual on L.M. Region 9Fs.   [David M. Cox]

•ther and sister from the same stable; a 'Britannia' Pacific and a Class 9 buffered up. The two
gns shared a great deal in common although there was not the degree of major standard-
•on a layman might expect.   [David M. Cox]

ontrast in front ends at Southall, September 1964—ex-G.W.R. 2-8-0 No. 3859 and 9F No.
45. The latter was one of the last Crewe batch (Nos. 92221-50), built in 1958 shortly before
works turned over completely to the construction of diesels.   [David M. Cox]

An overhead view of No. 92211: the massive 5′ 9″– 6′ 1″ diameter boiler meant that the Ross 'pop' safety valves on the rear barrel ring behind the steam dome had to be recessed. Of necessity, too, the steam dome was extremely squat. The steam manifold is prominent in the foreground on top of the firebox.

[David M. Cox]

The cab and nearside of No. 92089 at Horton Road shed, Gloucester, 30 January 1966. The design and layout of the spacious cab on the B. Standards were intended to to combine so far as possible all the best features from existing modern pre-Nationalisation classes; it wa. basically similar to that on th 'Britannias' but, unlike the latter, was attached to the frame and with a fall-plate in the normal way hinged over from the tender. The grimy work-worn condition No. 92089 was typical of 9F in service.

[Norman E. Pre.

The fireman's side of Crewe-built No. 92030, shed at Gloucester in October 1965. The sandl fillers can be seen above the running plate, th being on the right-hand side only. The two jectors are prominent below the cab on this s and the sanding gear can be seen at either side the main driver. [Norman E. Pree

No. 92085, at Southall, November 1963. This locomotive was withdrawn in November 1966.
[David M. Cox]

No. 92224, in unusually clean condition following a recent visit to the works, at Oxford. She is coupled to the inset 1G Class tender. The lack of flange on the nearside main driver is clearly seen. [L. Waters]

No. 92220 was the last steam locomotive built at Swindon and, named *Evening Star*, became justifiably celebrated on Western Region. She has been preserved and is seen here outside the paint shop at Crewe works on 15 January 1967.

[Norman E. Preedy]

Excessive motion lubrication and lack of cleaning add a heavy coating of oil and grease to wheels and running gear of No. 92146—hardly conducive to good traction of tyre on rail. T sandpipe ahead of the leading driver helps to make it all a good abrasive compound. Note steam-operated cylinder drain cocks.

[Norman E. Pree

22

A classic photograph of a 9F in action, No. 92058 on an up coal train emerging from Elstree Tunnel, 25 May 1957. On duties such as this, the new 2-10-0s had just displaced the long familiar Garratts that had been the motive power on coal trains along the Midland main line. By this date something like 140 9Fs were in service, and handling much of the freight turns on London Midland, Eastern and North Eastern Regions. With 39,667 lbs tractive effort, they could 'move mountains'.

[Brian Morrison]

A later 9F, No. 92227, with double chimney, photographed at Leamington Spa in August 1958, a month after entering service on Western Region. Most W.R. 9Fs had the smaller 1G tender with 7 tons coal capacity and inset coal box, which was sufficiently large for the Region's requirements.
[Brian Morrison]

gle chimney 9Fs in service on Eastern Region; No. 92038 plodding down the slow line near
tters Bar (above) and No. 92040 passing Hatfield (below). Both were coupled to 1F class tenders,
th flush sides. The five tender variations fitted to the 9Fs were 20 Class 1B, 85 each Class 1C
d 1F, 58 Class 1G and 3 Class K—the last three being the stoker-fitted variants.
[Norman E. Preedy]

No. 92079, completed at Crewe early in 1956 and originally allocated to Toton, was chosen to replace the well known 'Big Bertha' 0-10-0 used as the main banker on the Lickey incline. No. 92079, fitted with the latter's special headlight, is seen (left) at Swindon works and in action behind a northbound express in August 1962. [N. E. Preedy] She started work in May 1956 in company with eight 'Jinty' 0-6-0 tanks—the latter replaced by W.R. 84xx class panniers in 1958 when this section of line passed from L.M. to W. Region control. No. 92079 is seen (right) alongside the bankers' coal stage at Bromsgrove on 9 August 1956, and (below) assisting a passenger train near the top of Lickey on 16 January 1960. The headlight, intended to help at night when closing up to the rear of trains, had passed out of use by this date.

[P. J. Shoesmith]

at York; No. 92191 (above) on a down freight and No. 92177 (below) heading north. Both
e locomotives, built at Swindon and Crewe respectively, entered service in the spring of 1958.
92191 was withdrawn from service late in 1965 and No. 92177 even earlier, in May 1964.
h a short working life for steam locomotives illustrates how even such an efficient, easily
ntained class as the 9F was made redundant by the onset of total dieselisation. Eastern Region
the first to commence their withdrawal.   [Brian Morrison]

The ability of the new 2-10-0s to handle fast fitted freights equally as well as slow speed loose-coupled ones very
soon came to be appreciated, particularly on Eastern Region where there was a shortage of motive power
suitable for the former. Here, No. 92182 heads north from Hadley Wood tunnels on the G.N. main line with a
train of vans for Leeds, in July 1959.
                                                                          [Derek Cross]

No. 92054 on 19 April 1968, near the end of her days and only a matter of weeks from withdrawal, heads coal empties past Bamber Bridge, near Preston. Crewe-built in 1955, she was one of the last dozen or so to remain in service.

[David M. Cox]

Apart from major variations, the class changed little in detail despite their production being spread over a period of several years—a tribute to their original design. One minor modification was the addition of a large single step below the smokebox door instead of the two small ones originally fitted, as seen here on No. 92137.

[L. Waters]

...ouble-chimneyed No. 92227 running light at Copredy, near Banbury, 16 September 1966.
...e first allocation of 9Fs to Banbury was made in August 1958 for working iron ore trains to
...uth Wales—duties on which they replaced Stanier 8Fs. The smaller 1G class tenders were
...ovided on the locomotives here.

[David M. Cox]

By 1958 shedmasters had begun to discover that the 9Fs were useful on excursions and summer specials; despite 5′ diameter wheels, a few were even put on turns such as 'The Master Cutler' on the former Great Central line. Here No. 92009 approaches Lutterworth with the up 'South Yorkshireman' on 8 August 1959. [P. J. Shoesmith]

By 1959 Western Region had also discovered the capabilities of 9Fs to help out at summer weekends whe passenger traffic was at its height. No. 92243 (above) is on a Cardiff–Brighton train at Bathampton in July that year and No. 92223 (below) passing Dawlish has charge of a Paignton–Nottingham relief, in Septembe Considering the rarity of eight-coupled classes on passenger workings in Britain, the success of 2-10-0s in th sphere was indeed a considerable break with tradition.

[Derek Cros

Pressure on British Railways' passenger carrying capacity, both in motive power and rolling stock, was at the limit during summer months in the 1950s, in the era before the ownership of a car by almost every family. Lines to holiday areas such as the North Wales coast saw numerous seasonal 'extras', one of which—the 10.10 a.m. Sheffield–Bangor, draws away from Prestatyn on an afternoon in early September 1959.

[S. D. Wainwright]

Cross-country routes also saw the 9Fs in increasing numbers as the years passed, although at more mod authorised speeds than the 80s and 90s which the operating authorities had frowned upon in 1959. No. 920 passing Kidlington signal box near Oxford on 20 August 1966, is heading the 10.45 a.m. Bournemouth Newcastle—a heavy train over an undulating route for which a 9F was very well suited. [David M. C Below, No. 92051 from Saltley shed, leaving Derby (Midland) on a summer Saturday relief from the No Eastern Region, August 1957.

[P. J. Lyn

The major variation in the 251 Class 9Fs that were built was the batch of ten locomotives fitted with Crosti boilers, Nos. 92020-29. Strikes in the collieries plus the rapidly increasing cost of coal drove B.R. to a trial revision of the 9F design in the 1953 building programme to incorporate a preheater as a means of achieving an economy in coal consumption. A long feedwater heater, not unlike a second small boiler, ran beneath the main boiler barrel, the steam and smoke passing through this and then exhausting to the atmosphere through a chimney (or blast chamber) midway along the locomotive on the fireman's side. The Crostis came in in 1955 and tests in that year proved that the increase in efficiency was marginal compared to the extra building and maintenance costs of what had become a non-standard design in many ways. All ten in the series were allocated to Wellingborough shed in the East Midlands, for work on coal trains to and from Cricklewood. The close-up at Toton (left) shows the right-hand side of No. 92026 on 24 July 1955. [Brian Morrison] The Crostis were unpopular with shed staff and footplate crew alike, and they were out of service by 1958-59. Three of them are seen above at Wellingborough shed on 19 April 1959, stored until rebuilding could be arranged at works.
[Norman E. Preedy]

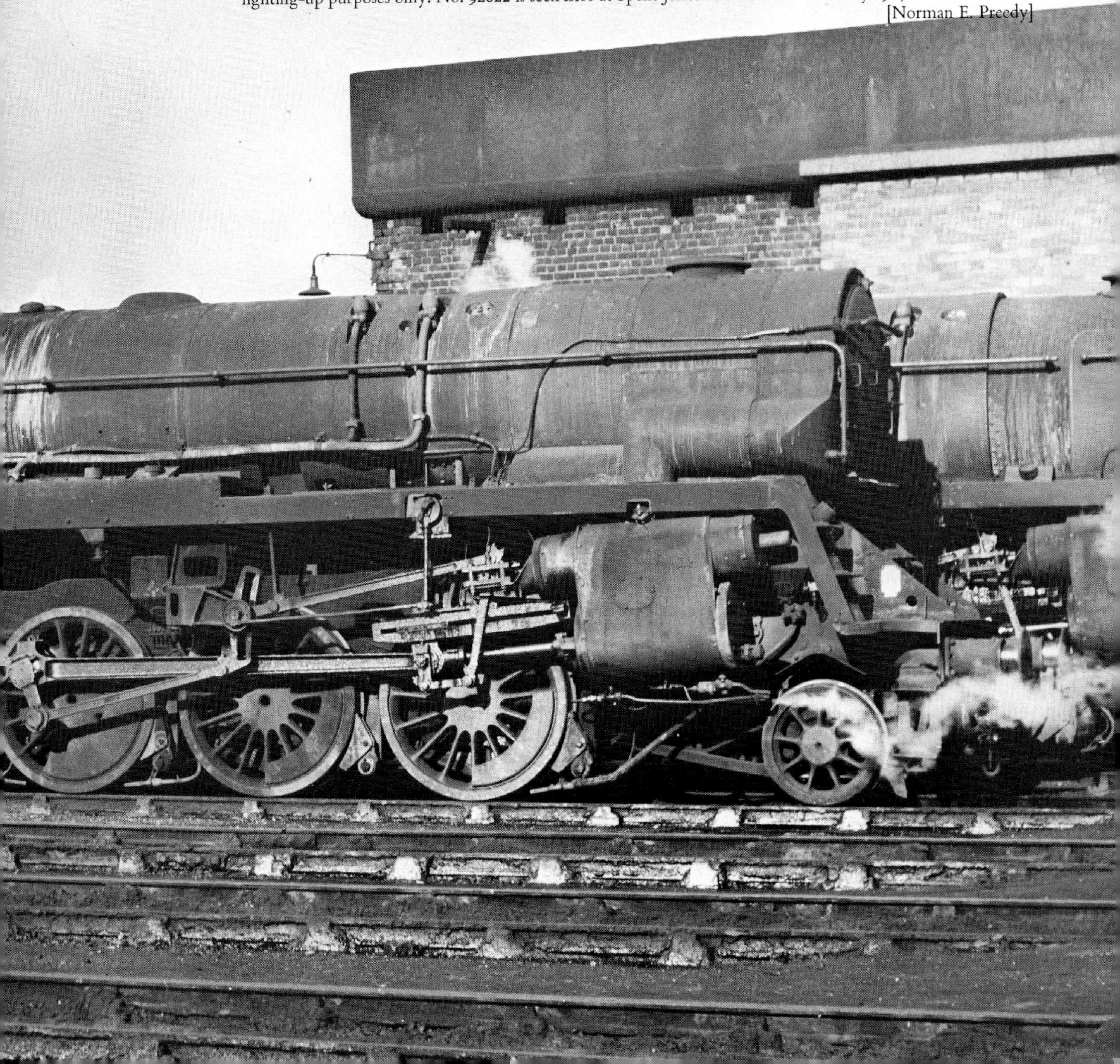

Last of the ten Crosti 9Fs to be re-boilered was No. 92022, in the spring of 1962 after a period of storage at Wellingborough whilst the other nine were rebuilt (from October 1959 onwards). The smaller diameter boiler was retained, with the preheater barrel beneath it removed, along with the associated pipework and supplementary chimney. The normal function of the latter was resumed; in the Crosti layout it had been retained for lighting-up purposes only. No. 92022 is seen here at Speke Junction shed on 18 February 1967.

[Norman E. Preedy]

Nos. 92028 and 92022 at Wellingborough in the mid-1950s. The deflectors by the after chimney helped somewhat to reduce the problem of smoke affecting the fireman's side of the cab. A major drawback on the Crostis was the lack of a self-cleaning smokebox, and the class was heartily disliked, by shed staff and footplate crews alike, for their dirtiness.

[Norman E. Preedy]

The front end of a Crosti was always cleaner than the smoke-begrimed after end; No. 92027, not long in service and still without deflector, approaching Elstree Tunnel on 7 July 1955.
[R. K. Taylor]

No. 92028, seen opposite in original form, after rebuilding in 1959. The high pitched boiler barrel, the bulges and blanked-off excrescences made the ex-Crostis rapidly identified, quite apart from their lack of smoke deflectors.
[R. H. Leslie]

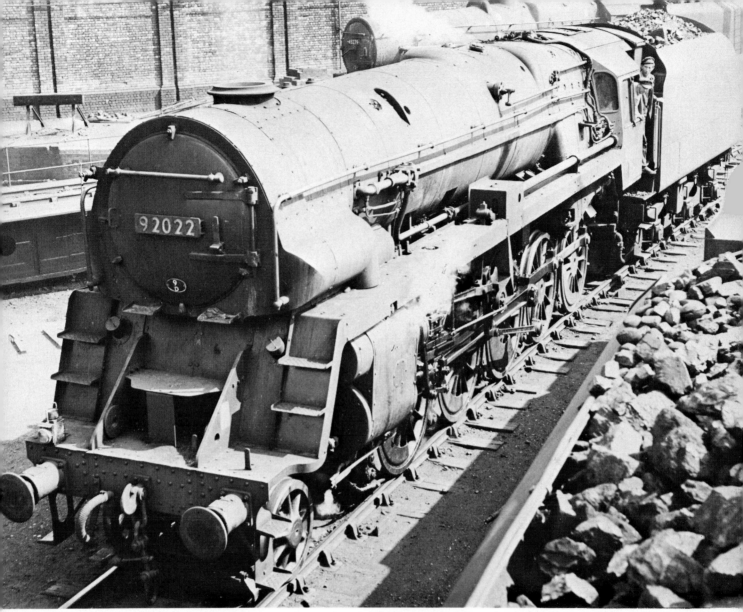

No. 92022 on shed at Patricroft, photographed from the tender of a Stanier 8F. [J. R. Carter]

M. Region retained the ten former Crosti variants after these had been restored to more con-
...tional form and they ranged far and wide on general freight duties until their withdrawal in
...57. No. 92027 here approaches Derby (Midland) with a southbound loose-coupled freight in
...ril 1963.
[P. J. Lynch]

No. 92028 outside Barrow Road shed at Bristol, 7 June 1965. All these ten variants were provided with 1B Class tenders. The sideraking doors of the ashpan are open, and clearly visible.   [David M. Cox]

The last of the 198 9Fs built at Crewe was No. 92250, completed in December 1958. She was also the last steam locomotive to be built there, heralding the change-over to the construction of diesels. Originally provided with a double chimney, No. 92250 later in 1959 had a Giesl multiple nozzle chimney fitted in the hope of securing a worthwhile economy in coal consumption. Allocated to W.R., No. 92250 went to Banbury for a time and then to Ebbw Junction. She is seen here at Didcot on 1 September 1964. Long and narrow, this Giesl 'ejector' looked sadly out of keeping atop such a handsome heavyweight as the 9F.   [David M. Cox]

A rebuilt Crosti with another of the conventional 9Fs alongside. Various points can be noted in this interesting comparison, including such details as the repositioned sandbox ahead of the cylinder (with forward facing filler), and a splash guard above the pony truck.

[Norman E. Preedy]

49

Coupled to a 1G inset tender, ex-Crosti No. 92024 clumps north past Kingmoor new yard at Carlisle in April 1965 with a Glasgow-bound train of limestone from Shap quarries.   [Derek Cross]

A string of coal empties behind No. 92025 at Elstree on the Midland main line, August 1960.   [Derek Cross

No. 92028, seen here running light at Tramway Junction, Gloucester, was the first of the ex-Crosti series to be withdrawn, in October 1966.

[W. L. Underhay

No. 92025 on the turntable at Crewe South shed, 15 July 1967. A clean 9F was a rare sight, their working lives being in the era when shed cleaners were in worse than short supply. [Norman E. Preedy]

No. 92001 passing Gloucester with a block train of Esso tank wagons. December 1965. By this date she had acquired a double chimney (fitted in 1958) in contrast to her original as depicted on pages 8-9. Only three locomotives were modified in this way. [P. J. Lynch]

indon-built No. 92215, with double chimney, was put into traffic in November 1959. She ted until 1967 but certain of this final Swindon batch saw service for little more than five years. is was but a fraction of their possible working life under normal conditions and made their lding cost, then amounting to more than £33,000, quite uneconomic. [David M. Cox]

Late evening sunlight emphasises the massive bulk of No. 92152, seen drifting through Kings Norton station with a W.R. brakevan in 1963. 5′ diameter wheels under a wide firebox meant the use of every millimetre of the loading gauge. It is not difficult to understand how the 9Fs came to have the nickname of 'spaceships'. [P. J. Shoesmith]

No. 92126 gets under way from Chester with a loose-coupled freight, 14 June 1966.
[W. L. Underhay]

Grimy, work-worn, and neglected though they might have been in the last year or so of steam, the 9Fs were still efficient and capable; No. 92054 near Preston in April 1968. [David M. Cox]

Steam to spare on No. 92082, getting a heavy train of petrol tanks under way at Huddersfield, 28 October 1967. With 77½ tons weight on ten-coupled drivers, 9Fs could walk away without fear of slipping. Total engine and tender weight was about 140 tons, varying slightly with the class of tender.

[P. J. Lynch]

st freights were a *forte* of the 9Fs, and a duty for which they were ideal; No. 92009, near Oxen-
olme, 28 July 1967.   [David M. Cox]

Another fully fitted freight on the main line over Shap—No. 92051 in the Lune Valley near Tebay on 10 June
1967. None of the Regions had a locomotive class that was such a good all-rounder as the 9F, which served B.R.
extremely well in the decade or so after 1955.
                                                                       [R. H. Leslie]

Scottish Region had a few 9Fs for a time, whilst numerous L.M. and N.E. allocated ones worked there; No. 92022 on the curve through Lamington in the rural valley of the Clyde with a southbound goods, May 1964.

[Derek Cross]

duty on which 9Fs became extremely well known was the working of anhydrite trains over the Settle & arlisle route from Long Meg quarries near Appleby to Widnes in south Lancashire. These weighty hopper ains became the province of the class, and made up some of the heaviest freights worked over Ais Gill. No. 2019 (above) is just past the summit on the long run downhill through Kirkby Stephen. Below, coming south ith a loaded train, No. 92076 passes Blea Moor loops on 19 June 1965 amid the typically desolate but beautiful enery of these northern fells.

[Derek Cross]

Little sign of the adverse gradient is apparent from No. 92052 leisurely taking a northbound train of empty stock up past Scout Green towards Shap summit, 19 August 1966. The crew of the 2-6-4T banker behind her thirteen-coach load evidently have little steam on and are not far from receiving a tow to the summit.

[R. H. Leslie]

To suit operating requirements and also when moved from one Region to the allocation of another, various of the class acquired different tenders from the ones specified at the time of building. No. 92118, originally provided with a 9 ton 1C tender, was running with the 1G inset type in 1967, as seen here at Shipley in Yorkshire on 2 May of that year.

[Norman E. Preedy]

Another 9F on Shap; No. 92025—looking as functionally ugly as only a rebuilt Crosti could—passing Scout Green box with a Warrington - Carlisle freight. [J. R. Carter]

A view along the running plate of No. 92049, photographed from the footplate on a Patricroft - St. Helens freight near Astley Green in June 1966.

[J. R. Carter]

Downholme, close beside the river Lune on the north side of Tebay, was a photographer's paradise in the days of steam, particularly for northbound trains which were getting away again up Shap after a stop for the banker. Here the driver has the regulator full open on No. 92055 in May 1966, as he gets under way again for Carlisle.

[Norman E. Preedy]

No. 92218 fights for her feet on a greasy rail at Banbury on a cold morning in December 1965. [David M. Cox]

No. 92001 again, at Shepton Mallet with three coaches and a parcels van forming the the 9.05 a.m. Bristol to Bournemouth, 29 August 1962. Due to lack of steam heating, the 9Fs were confined to summer working on the S. & D.

[W. L. Underhay]

The effect of over-exuberant speeds on passenger working with 9Fs brought an official ban on their use in this capacity except in emergencies. This was a result of the greatly reduced period between overhauls that the class needed if they had much high speed use. With a heavy passenger train over a hilly route, however, it was another matter and the 9Fs were tried out on the Somerset & Dorset Bath-Bournemouth route from 1960 onwards with conspicuous success. Here No. 92001, at Masbury summit in July of that year, has charge of a Leeds-Bournemouth extra.

[Derek Cross]

No. 92245, on 28 June 1962, bursts out of the tunnel at Midford with a southbound train on the S & D. Prior to the introduction of the 9Fs the maximum load for a Class 5 without a pilot had been eight bogies, and the same for the 'West Country' Pacifics, which were badly prone to slipping. The S. & D. 2-8-0s were allowed ten on at times when they too were pressed into passenger service, whilst the 9Fs were rostered to take up to twelve. On the heaviest turns such as 'The Pines Express', the 2-10-0s did some fine work on the hard grades of this interesting cross-country route.   [Derek Cross]

The 9F allocation at Banbury became standard motive power on the iron ore trains through to South Wales; No. 92218 leaves the former in December 1965 at the head of a train of hoppers. [David M. Cox]

The principal value of the 1G Class tender with its inset coal bunker was to help sighting when running tender first—though it was rare to see a 9F working any main line train in this fashion: No. 92227 near Copredy with a train of 36 empty ore hoppers, 16 September 1966. [David M. Cox]

Iron ore again, passing Lansdown Junction at Cheltenham bound for the Margam steel mills, in tipplers behind No. 92150, 10 June 1964. [Derek Cross]

By the early 1960s, with all 251 of the 2-10-0s in service, they had become a common sight on heavy freight duty everywhere, exceeded only in some areas by the more numerous Stanier 8Fs. Here two 9Fs cross at Horton Road, Gloucester—both Crewe-built but showing variations within the class; No. 92139, built in 1957, has the more common single chimney and 1C tender; No. 92228, built in 1958, has the double chimney and smaller 1G tender.   [Norman E. Preedy]

One of the freight duties with which the 9Fs will always be associated was the Consett iron ore trains on N.E. Region, on which they replaced Class 01 2-8-0s. The first 9Fs went there at the end of 1955, to Tyne Dock shed, and early the following year they were fitted with Westinghouse pumps for working air-operated discharge doors on the bogie hoppers used for this traffic. No. 92064, one of the Tyne Dock 9Fs, is seen (above and opposite) working one of these trains made up of the usual nine wagons—a trailing load, with brake van, of almost 800 tons.   [David M. Cox]

No.92097 in semi-silhouette, hard at work near Stanley on one of the succession of trains up from Tyne Dock staithes to the furnaces of the Consett Iron Co., 7 May 1963. Three sets of nine wagons were used in the service on a circuit system, with as many as ten trains a day worked between the port and the steel works.

[A. R. Butcher]

Very steep gradients
required the help of a
banker on the final
climb to Consett; No
92061 draws into Sou
Pelaw with an up trai
and passes No. 92062
waiting ready for this
duty. Note the air
compressors let in to
offside running plate.
[Malcolm Dun

Nos. 92060–66 and
92097–99 remained at
Tyne Dock until 1966
when they were with-
drawn and Class 24
diesel-electrics took ov
the working of the or
trains; Nos. 92097 and
92099 inside Tyne Do
shed, 17 August 1966.
[David M. C

In addition to normal heavy freight use, Western Region 9Fs probably saw more varied duties than those on any other region, varying from passenger specials to places such as Paignton in summer, to milk trains and even —for a brief fling—on expresses such as the Cardiff-London 'Capitals United'; No. 92245 (above) slams through Starcross station in Devon with an up milk train from Cornwall in July 1960. [W. L. Underhay]

No. 92241 heads west through Sonning Cutting with a motley collection of empty coaching stock in August 1960. Forward visibility on the 9Fs past the massive boiler, high-set running plate and wide smoke deflectors, was not good; on Western Region routes, sighting signals and the road ahead was made somewhat worse by their left-hand drive—as with 'Britannias'—compared to the traditional 'offside' position for driving standard GWR locomotives. [Derek Cross]

No. 92236 at Oxford, awaiting the road out to Hinksey, 23 May 1962. Her driver, lost in thought, ponders over the coming of diesel-hydraulics . . . or perhaps on the pros and cons of locomotives with left-hand drive . . . [J. R. Besley]

No. 92203, completed at Swindon in March 1959, served on L.M. Region and was one of the considerable batch of 9Fs withdrawn towards the end of 1967. Some months later she was bought by David Shepherd, the artist renowned for wild-life and locomotive portraiture, for preservation. Named *Black Prince* and restored to pristine condition, this magnificent 9F, seen here at Eastleigh on an Open Day in March 1972, is now the principal attraction at Cranmore.

[Norman E. Preedy]

No. 92203 in Crewe South depot, out of service and surrounded by diesel shunters, 30 December 1967.

[Norman E. Preedy]

A rail-level view of Swindon-built No. 92211 at Oxford on 21 March 1965. She was one of five of the c
allocated in the early 1960s to Southern Region, and shedded at Eastleigh (71a). They were intended for work
heavy oil trains, principally to the Midlands, from the refinery at Fawley near Southampton. Subseque
they were transferred to Feltham and from there, finally, to Eastern Region at York. No. 92211 was w
drawn in May 1967.

[David M. C

A pair of W.R. 9Fs at Aberbeeg in the Welsh valleys. With a 21′ 8″ coupled wheel base, these decapods were limited on the curves they could negotiate but the flangeless main (central) driver enabled them to take 400′ radius curves and even down to 300′, dead slow, on sidings.

[Norman E. Preedy]

A nearside view of No. 92214 on Swindon shed, 24 September 1964. Reasonable quality coal, or a reasonable quality fireman, was needed to get the best out of a 9F if it was to be worked really hard; two firemen, rather than one, were needed for sustained output anywhere near the limit of the design and three 9Fs (Nos. 92165-67) were experimentally fitted with Berkley mechanical stokers in 1958, but results in service were disappointing.

[David M. Cox]

92046 on the
ntable at Leeds
olbeck) shed, 2 May
57.   [David M. Cox]

Most famous of the 9Fs is No. 92220 *Evening Star*, now preserved. Almost too well known to need description, she was the last steam locomotive built at Swindon and was turned out in 1960 in green livery, with copper-capped double chimney and with nameplates on the smoke deflectors. The name, chosen as a result of a naming competition among W.R. staff, was an apt one and also recalled one from the old G.W.R. days.

[David M. Cox]

Allocated as one of the stud of 9Fs at Cardiff (Canton), No. 92220—though something of a 'pet'—was rostered for run-of-the-mill work when not earmarked for the occasional special duty, as witness her on a freight at Gloucester Central on 19 November 1964. She was often to be seen on Cardiff - Brighton trains and also headed the last 'Pines Express' over the Somerset & Dorset in September 1962.

[Norman E. Preedy]

Evening Star in Newport (Ebbw Junction) shed, 15 April 1964. B.R. had earmarked her for preservation and she was withdrawn in March 1965. This was after only five years of active service, the shortest of any in the class. After languishing in store in a state of limbo for some time, *Evening Star* was given an overhaul and repaint at Crewe in the winter of 1966-67 and can now be seen in action again, on the Keighley & Worth Valley line in Yorkshire.

[David M. Cox]

No. 92051 has her tender refilled at Carlisle (Kingmoor), one of the last strongholds of the class, 29 April 1967. The 1C class tender carried 4725 gallons of water, as with the externally similar 1B class, but nine tons of coal compared to seven with the latter—the basic difference being simply the length of the interior coal space. With the nine-tonner, the back seldom got cleared of a great deal of vintage slack that, with age, became more and more unburnable.   [David M. Cox]

90

A 9F undergoing overhaul at Eastleigh works, 1 May 1965. By this date both Crewe and Swindo were devoted solely to diesel manufacture. Below, No. 92179, ex-Eastleigh works in March 196 hauled by the Eastleigh shed pilot.   [David M. Cox

A melancholy duty for a 9F; No. 90226 hauling ex-Southern Moguls and a Standard 2-6-4T 'dead - own wheels' through Gloucester *en route* to scrap yards in South Wales, 28 June 1965.   [Norman E. Preedy]

An unusual trio on the main line north of Banbury; a pair of 9Fs (Nos. 92129 and 92118) making a sandwich of a North Eastern B1.   [David M. Cox]

Some of the last batch of withdrawn 9Fs at Carnforth shed in June 1968. Among the eight are Nos. 92088 (foreground, with 1F Class tender) 92091 and 92167 (centre). The latter was one of the trio fitted with mechanical stoker from 1958-62, and was also the last of the class to be officially withdrawn. Curious to relate, her final few weeks were without rear coupling rods (as can be seen in this photograph), though how far she ran as a temporary 2-8-2 is not known. [David M. Cox]

End of the line for former No. 92050, newly arrived at a breaker's yard in Newport in March 1968—101 tons or so of good quality scrap. Times had changed since this 9F was first steamed at Crewe back in the autumn of 1955; the last class of British-built main line steam had come and gone; another few months and there would be nothing left in day-to-day service except diesels.

[Norman E. Preedy]

A 9F running on B.R. metals again; *Black Prince* heading a rail tour near Oxford in 1973. As already noted, this locomotive is now at Cranmore in Somerset, in black livery and beautifully maintained; many will agree that, along with *Evening Star*, she is amongst the most impressive preserved locomotives in Britain. [L. Waters]

A striking study of No. 92220 *Evening Star* on the Keighley & Worth Valley Railway in West Yorkshire, 1973. The two preserved 9Fs are enduring memorials to one of the finest—albeit short-lived—locomotive classes ever seen in this country.   [J. R. Carter]

acknowledgments: the editor and publishers wish to thank the many photographers whose work appears in this volume and without whom it could not have been compiled.